INSTANT CONNECTION

Instant Connection

The INSTANT-Series *Presents*

INSTANT

CONNECTION

How to Build Rapport with Anyone Instantly!

Instant Series Publication

Copyright © Instant Series Publication

All rights reserved.

It is impermissible to reproduce any part of this book without prior consent. All violations will be prosecuted to the fullest extent of the law.

While attempts have been made to verify the information contained within this publication, neither the author nor the publisher assumes any responsibility for errors, omissions, interpretation or usage of the subject matter herein.

This publication contains the opinions and ideas of its author and is intended for informational purpose only. The author and publisher shall in no event held liable for any loss or other damages incurred from the usage of this publication.

ISBN 978-1-508-88243-5

Printed in the United States of America

First Edition

FIRST STEP:

Before proceeding, visit http://www.instantseries.com, and join the **INSTANT Newsletter** now.

You will want to! :)

Instant Connection

CONTENTS

Chapter 1 - We All Want to Connect with Others

11 - Lost In Connection

13 - The Need For Open Channel

14 - Things To Take Into Considerations

Chapter 2 - What Can You Do to Build Instant Connection

16 - Learn To Build Rapport

18 - All About The Eyes

20 - Practice Eye Contacts

21 - Confidence Dominates All

23 - Practice Confidence

25 - Empathetic Connecting

30 - Practice Questioning

31 - Handle Boring Interaction

33 - Fake It Until You Like It

35 - Task: Connect With Someone

Chapter 3 - How to Become Somebody who Makes Connections Easily

37 - Developing Socially

38 - Attributes Of Easy Connecting

39 - What's To Come

Chapter 4 - How to Practice in the Art of Rapport

41 - Exercise: I Love You Mirror

42 - Exercise: Confidence All Over

43 - Laughter Is Ultimate Ingredient Of Rapport

44 - Exercise: Work On Your Humor

47 - Utilize Social Savviness

48 - Exercise: Record What's Interesting About You

Chapter 5 - How to Keep a Connection

54 - Once The Connection Is Made

56 - Putting In Maintenance

Chapter 6 - Start Creating Connections Now

59 - Past To Present

60 - Connecting The Dots

Instant Connection

Instant Connection

Chapter 1

We All Want to Connect with Others

Lost In Connection

If you've ever thought about **connecting with others**, it might, at first glance, have seemed like a skill that just comes naturally...

But if you've ever watched two toddlers interacting, this comfortable theory gets pretty much shot to pieces.

If you've ever paid attention at a gathering or an ordinary social call, you've probably noticed how rare it is for two little kids to get along at first sight. Symptoms are pretty much universal: they'll stare at one another for a while, try making tentative eye contact, then look away quickly or retreat to a parent's lap. Even if they really want a new friend, they may just end up ignoring each other for the entire visit.

Then why do they do it?

The answer? They just don't know how to connect with others yet.

For most people, *wanting* to connect socially is a natural born instinct, but that doesn't mean it's something we're all born *knowing* how to do immediately.

Generally, (if we're lucky) we're taught these social skills by parents, teachers, or other role models before we become official "grown-ups". So learning "social skills" might seem simple and straightforward, something you'd teach a three year-old.

But if we're going to be honest, some people, even in their middle age, still haven't mastered these skills.

The Need For Open Channel

If you're one of those people who has difficulty making a good connection with others, this isn't a definite indicator that you're "anti-social" or you don't want to interact. In truth, you probably just lack the skills you need to make it happen.

Besides that, connections can be difficult to quantify.

For example, in a one-sided friendship you may not feel at all connected to someone, while they see something in you that they share, a special energy, if you will.

This is a more common problem than you might suppose. Many marriages have fallen apart because one spouse lacked that special connection, while the other was unaware of the problem.

Often it can also be difficult to decide just how much of a connection there actually is between two people.

Simple words such as "*like*" and "*love*" are really the only words we have to describe these connections, but such words are completely abstract. It's hard to find a concrete way to express such feelings.

Things To Take Into Considerations

There are a few things that you have to consider when you're faced with new connections, things such as:

- Why do you want to make this connection?

- Are you confident that the other person wants to make the connection as well?

- Do you feel you have the skills to create a lasting friendship, work relationship or romantic relationship with this person?

These questions are important and merit some close consideration. They're going to shape the way you interact, and help you create and maintain a connection.

One of the most important things to keep in mind here is that **a connection requires two people**. This may seem like a statement of the obvious, but if you're going to overcome all the difficulties of building a connection, both people need to be completely committed to it and both need to be working toward the same end goal.

Chapter 2
What Can You Do to Build Instant Connection

Learning Rapport Building

Have you ever noticed how some people seem to connect naturally and easily, while others are completely lacking in those same social and emotional skills? It seems like a completely unfair balance, doesn't it?

But look at it reasonably for a minute. Sure, some people may have an innate sense that helps them relate to others, but that's not the only factor you need to be looking at here. Some people may be born with a little more tact and skill in this area, but they still had to learn and develop the actual technique just like anybody else.

Don't feel discouraged when you see someone who's better at this than you. Instead, you should feel encouraged, because if they were able to practice and improve to such an extent, you should be able to do it too, right?

Social skills, as mentioned before, are *learned behaviors*.

You teach your children, and even your pets, how to behave in a variety of social situations, so similarly, you should be able to reach yourself as well.

But before you rush out and grab a stranger to practice your social skills on, there are a few simple habits you have to consider and learn.

Some of them may seem pretty obvious, but you'd be amazed how many people ignore them on a regular basis.

All About The Eyes

First and foremost, you've got to make (and maintain) **eye contact.**

This advice is pretty much common sense. But even though *you* may be thinking "*Duh!*" this isn't a technique people always take advantage of.

As a matter of fact, you've probably noticed that the more you WANT to connect with someone, the less easy it is to make eye contact. There's pretty much a direct correlation between how much you want to meet someone and how shy you are about it. In reality, this is because the more you want to meet someone, the more worried you are about making a good impression, and the more awkward and nervous you become.

Think about it.

Do you remember ever moving to a new grade in school, or to a new neighborhood? There was that one kid there that you were dying to meet, but you never could bolster your courage enough to introduce yourself.

The technical explanation for this is simply that you desperately wanted to connect, but you felt too insecure to do so.

The lesson to learn from this is: if you want to connect with anyone *(your significant other, your child, your boss, your friend, whoever!)*...you have to begin by looking them directly in the eye and continuing to do so as you speak.

Make no mistake, you're probably going to find this much more difficult than you would have thought, and it *will* require practice, but the payoff will be worth it.

To start yourself off, first pay close attention to your own habits when you're speaking to people.

- Do you look them in the eye, or over their shoulder, at your feet, or dig through your purse to avoid contact?

- Do you stare at your phone or pay most of your attention to the TV?

That's one of the easiest ways NOT to connect with a person.

Practice Eye Contacts

To practice building this habit, begin by looking everyone you meet in the eye, even if you're not always trying to make a connection.

- Look the teller at the bank in the eye.

- Make eye contact with the clerk at the store.

- Whoever you meet, meet with your eyes too.

This practice will help you gain more confidence and make eye contact a little less intimidating.

If you need extra practice, you can even try practicing on yourself in the mirror. If this process seems a little silly, that may actually help you even more. Try and think of the extra embarrassment as extra practice.

Again, it's probably going to be a more difficult task than you would've thought, but just keep at it, because you *will* see results.

Confidence Dominates All

When it comes to making connections, **confidence** is key.

There's nothing more important than showing yourself as a secure individual with a good sense of self, but of course, this doesn't always come naturally in social situations.

There's nothing more natural than feeling nervous about a new connection. But if you want it to be a success, you're going to have to learn to overcome this feeling. There's no way to make a good connection if the first thing the other person sees about you is your weaknesses and insecurity. And even if you do manage to make a connection, chances are you're not going to be thrilled with the relationship that develops. If a person sees your weaknesses before anything else, he's going to find it difficult to respect you, and respect is another key factor of a good relationship.

If you truly want connection and social interaction, you've got to be willing to actively pursue it and be confident that you can create and maintain the other person's friendship or love or whatever relationship you're looking to make.

For example, if you need your boss to see and acknowledge your worth around the office, whether you're looking for a raise or just a little recognition, you have to be able to make him respect you. Avoiding contact with him, acting nervous or averting your eyes and fidgeting when he talks to you doesn't exactly give you an appearance of confidence. If you look him in the eye, talk to him as an equal, and sound sure of what you're saying, you're going to show him qualities that he can admire. If he's looking for someone to promote to management, for instance, then he's going to look for someone who he can trust to handle any problems that come along, somebody confident.

Or, if you want to be romantically involved with someone, appearing nervous or unsure around them may seem cute at first, but it's going to get old fast.

Be confident and sure of who you are. There's nothing more likely to gain people's attention and make them want to get to know you. If you're not comfortable with who you are, why should they be?

Practice Confidence

Even if you don't naturally feel confident, the illusion of confidence works just as well and at the same time helps make *real* confidence come more easily. Also known as the *"fake it 'til you make it"* method.

You have numerous options for helping yourself appear confident – even when you're not. One of the quickest ways to gain confidence is as easy as a fashion makeover. Literally. Giving yourself something different, something that brings out the best in your looks, automatically makes you more confident in yourself, and more confident that others will see the best in you too.

Practice standing up straight and tall; take pictures of yourself in a mirror making your most confident face. Then do your hair and your clothes in a way that matches whatever it is that face most represents to you.

The point is, confidence cannot be built by anyone else, and making social connections is not something that can be done for you. *You* have to begin the process.

- If you see a fierce warrior princess when you look in the mirror, then obviously you need to go out and buy yourself a leopard print dress.

- If you look at your reflection and see an intelligent, capable man worthy of promotion, go out and get yourself a power suit. (A superhero suit might work too, it all depends.)

Your outward appearance does a lot toward defining who you are. Don't forget though, it's not being physically perfect that's so important.

What's truly magnetic is an attitude that's positive and electric. That all comes from one place: **high self-esteem**.

Empathetic Connecting

When you attempt to connect with others, **asking questions** is of paramount importance.

Think about it, when people meet you, do they ask you about yourself? Do they truly seem interested in getting to know you better? If they do, it's a good feeling, you know that they are actually interested in you. If they *don't*, it's hard to feel cared about, and chances are when you feel this way, you're right and there's not much future in an immediate connection.

But it works both ways. When you're meeting someone for the first time, are you truly interested in their answers? If you are, let them know it. They'll feel much more at home, and making the connection will become that much easier.

But when you ask other people questions, you've got to be careful, because a lot of times people mistake genuine interest for being nosy and prying.

The ability *to ask the right questions* is rooted in **empathy** – you have to pay attention to the way the other person feels, and pay attention to the subtle cues he gives you.

It's easy to tell when a conversation has been mortally wounded by boredom or lack of interest. It's also pretty simple to know when you've offended the other party or hurt them by something you've said without thinking.

It's your reaction, what you do when these things happen, that will define your connection.

If you notice signs of boredom when you're discussing something with the other person, or you can tell that discussing it makes them uncomfortable or unhappy, there's a simple remedy: change the subject!

It's kind of a "Duh!" statement, but you'd be surprised how often people overlook it when they're overeager to make a connection.

Rather than stopping an uncomfortable, awkward, or boring conversation, they continue to desperately push on in the vain hope of somehow resuscitating the rapport.

Knowing when the time has come to drop a topic requires you to pay less attention to yourself and be more attuned to the other person's feelings and reactions.

A car salesman is a good illustration for what we're talking about here. If you're looking for a used SUV and he's trying to pique your interest in an expensive luxury car that you really can't afford, he's going to be out of luck. If he pays enough attention to you and can tell that you aren't going to be convinced, a good salesman knows he's got to change tack.

Does it make sense to continue pushing the subject? Will this keep you interested, or will it alienate you?

Alienate you, right?

The truth is, once a salesman realizes you're just not interested, or you can't afford what he's offering, he should attempt to sell you something you *can* afford.

If you want to put the question of making a good connection in terms that apply in this example, you could say that when you're trying to make a connection, you're essentially "selling" yourself. This doesn't mean that your relationship is going to be sordidly based on money, it just means that you have to be able to offer a potential relationship that the other person wants.

In other words, you don't have to be a car salesman to use this method, it's just as useful in social negotiations as well. That's right...*negotiations.*

All relationships are essentially negotiated between two people and are the result of a specific dynamic.

If you meet a potential new friend that you'd love to develop a connection with, then you need to be ready to see them immediately for who they are so you can figure out how to make the friendship work.

If you're a football fanatic, for example, but the new friend would rather be forced to listen to a discourse on earthworms than football gossip, talking incessantly about football or leaving ESPN on TV the whole time they're around is going to alienate them very quickly. Worse than just becoming boring, you're ignoring *their* interests completely.

In this example, it would be more useful to sound out their interests and find something that you both enjoy talking about, something you can share.

Pushing your own interests, hobbies, beliefs or feelings onto someone else is the quickest way to push them away.

Practice Questioning

In order to practice this, you may want to carefully consider your own interests, beliefs, values and hobbies, and become aware of what matters most to you. That way, when people come into your life you can share about what you like, what you feel, and what you think.

However, it's just as important to be ready to turn the conversation to them, to ask questions about their life, and let *them* share what's important to them.

There's no time soon enough to start practicing this. It's a thing every person you meet can appreciate.

Ask everyone you come in contact with **ONE question**. It can be anything from how many children they have to what their favorite college basketball team is.

The point is to show an interest in the people around you. The more you ask questions and speak with people about their own lives, the easier it will become to show genuine interest in others.

Handle Boring Interaction

This brings us to our next point…what do you do if the topic of conversation just isn't something you appreciate?

The problem is that sometimes you very much want to connect with someone, but the conversation you're having isn't really very engaging for you.

We've covered what to do to engage them, but what happens if that engagement ends up in a conversation that you personally find pretty boring?

This may sound bad…but you'll probably have to *fake it*. You don't have to fake it every time or with every person, of course, but there are going to be plenty of times when you're going to have to try to show interest in things you don't care about.

This can be particularly important in the workplace. Think about it. You're constantly surrounded by people you may or may not share interests or beliefs with. It's a situation you can't do anything to change, but you do have to learn how to handle it. Making good connections at work is integral to long-term career success, and connecting well with people is one of the best ways to start.

The other thing you may find, if you encourage even the initially boring conversations, is that you actually *do* have something in common with the other party, something to discuss, or you may find that they have a quality in them that you can admire.

Fake It Until You Like It

Just like anything else, there are simple methods for pretending you're engaged in a boring conversation. We're going to focus on two here.

The first is to "fake it 'til you make it." The second is to smile and nod and maintain eye contact (we'll call this the **"grin and bear it"** method).

You may recall that the first method is the same one we discussed in regard to building self-confidence, but it's one that can used in almost any aspect of life. Since you're not always going to be fascinated by what people have to say, you can always pretend until you run into something that truly does interest you.

You may try to gently steer the conversation toward something of interest, but while you do so, you should maintain eye contact, smile, and nod. (Just make sure you don't overdo the nodding, because it's easy to end up looking and feeling like an insincere bobble-head toy.)

Smiling and nodding may sound like the simplest thing in the world, but it will make the other person feel acknowledged and heard, even if you don't have anything to add to the conversation.

We've already covered how important eye contact is to establishing connections, just remember that it's important in maintaining a conversation as well.

<u>Task</u>: Connect With Someone

If you want your connection to be a success, you need to practice in order to make these a habit when you're engaging with someone.

You can do this by looking in a mirror, just like you did when you worked on your eye contact.

You should also practice with people. Doing it just by yourself may help, but it doesn't really prepare you for actual personal contact. This may sound crazy, but you should try to actively seek out people you don't feel you have much in common with and attempt to start up a conversation. (You don't have to grab a stranger off the street, just someone you've never felt a connection to.)

There are two great reasons to do this: the first is that you may actually learn that you have more similarities than you would have previously thought, and the second is that this will provide you with the best opportunity to actually put into practice the skills previously discussed.

Today, while you're out and about, talk to at least one person who looks or acts differently than you.

It's amazing the common ground you can find with people, and the practice you'll get in building connections will be invaluable.

The truth is, all relationships are negotiations, and when you're attempting to connect with someone, you have to be willing to "grin and bear" certain things for the sake of the relationship.

Chapter 3

How to Become Somebody who Makes Connections Easily

Developing Socially

While you may be able to become more skilled with practice, building rapport probably still doesn't come easily to you. *If it did*, chances are you wouldn't be reading this.

It can be embarrassing to admit that you lack the social skills to make friends or engage with people.

This is because we tend to assume social skills come naturally, and if we don't have them, or have trouble using them, we're somehow inadequate.

<u>This is not the case.</u>

You have to keep in mind the example of preschool kids we used before. It will help remind you that everyone has to develop these skills. Besides, if a preschooler can do it, why can't you?

Attributes Of Easy Connecting

If you pay attention to people who seem to easily connect with others, you'll begin to see a pattern:

- They show interest, engage, smile, nod, make eye contact and speak easily and freely with others.

- They know that relationships are **give-and-take,** and they're willing to *"grin and bear"* a boring conversation for the sake of building a bridge between themselves and another person.

- They're confident and present themselves with ease.

- They stand up straight and look others in the eye.

If you've been reading carefully, you'll notice that they're mostly simple and straightforward techniques, the same ones previously discussed.

What's To Come

Here we'll have a more in-depth discussion of what you can do to practice these skills every day, and become better for it in the long run.

There are many things you can do to work on these skills, but you'll also need to be prepared to put yourself out there and be committed to your goal of connecting with new people.

Try to view this next chapter as homework. You have to be ready to do your part, if you want to succeed in becoming the person you want to see. Don't expect others to come to you. Go to them, and you may even find that they're willing to meet you halfway.

Use the skills that you'll gain from these assignments to find ways to bring people to you.

Chapter 4

How to Practice in the Art of Rapport

Exercise: I Love You Mirror

The first exercise you can try is similar to one we've already discussed: look in a mirror daily.

Try this for 5 minutes at a time, preferably (for you), when no one else is around. You'll more than likely feel silly or awkward, but keep at it all the same.

Practice your eye contact, your confident appearance, your smiling and nodding; you could even practice talking and asking questions. All the things we laid out above are techniques you can practice in the mirror.

If you do it every day, before work or school, it won't be long before you'll begin to see changes in your demeanor, ones that make you look more pleasant, agreeable, and more approachable altogether.

<u>Exercise</u>: Confidence All Over

The second exercise is to practice your confident walk.

You cannot possibly overestimate the importance of standing up straight and looking tall and proud.

Sure, you've probably been told since you were a kid to "stand up straight" and "don't slouch", but it wasn't just about keeping your back straight and improving your posture. It's all about making yourself seen and being confident.

To practice this, try walking around the house with a book on your head.

If you're a woman, put on high heels. They lend you inches and a more confident posture. You should also try doing this in front of a full-length mirror if possible. You'll be shocked at how little attention you usually pay to your physical carriage and your posture.

Aerobics or dance classes are another great way to get a feel for your body and gain confidence in your walk and your presence. If you don't want to sign up for classes, try buying a video for home use. Just like anything else, practice is the key here. If you end up walking like a super-model, don't say we didn't warn you.

Laughter Is Ultimate Ingredient Of Rapport

There's nothing better than humor for breaking ice.

Yeah, yeah, you probably think you don't have a funny bone in your body. But think about it again. Did you think you could gain confidence or find a common ground to talk about (or at least fake) with people, no matter who they are? If you can learn those things, what's to stop you from learning to amuse people?

For example, stand-up comedians' job is to make people to laugh, and they worry just as much as you do, but they still get up on stage and make jokes. And most of the time they're successful, even though they're nervous.

Why? Because their goal is to connect with others and make people happy. And it's something they enjoy, no matter how much they initially worry.

Humor is one of life's escapes, and everyone welcomes a connection with someone who can give them that.

<u>Exercise</u>: Work On Your Humor

It may sound strange, but there are actually exercises you can use to become funnier. In other words, you can work on practicing your jokes and becoming more at ease with humor.

The first technique is to **study comedians**. Watch funny movies or stand-up specials, and pay attention to how they crack their jokes and interact with the audience.

You may notice that usually they're funny without even "telling jokes." Don't worry, you don't have to get up on a stage in order to be funny, but this *is* something that you'll have to develop within your unique character. You can't just tell a joke and expect to become an instant magnet. You have to have a humorous "style" that matches the jokes and keeps people entertained.

But the best way to do this is to practice with jokes you're already familiar with and that you find amusing. If you're truly entertained by your jokes, you'll feel more natural being humorous around others.

How do you practice telling jokes? You guessed it: <u>in the mirror</u>.

Find about 10 jokes you find amusing, but make sure they're diverse enough to fit different people and contexts. This way, you'll be prepared for any situation, and can be the life of any party.

If you feel shy about introducing a joke, just remember, the more laughs you get, the easier it'll be to move away from "scripted" jokes to making your own.

In general, people find true-life situations funnier than a scripted joke. This is a common theme in comedies. The more people can relate to a funny story, joke, or plot, the more they'll laugh, and the more they'll enjoy it.

This is why a comedian often uses real life on stage...but with his own humorous spin. It's what makes us laugh.

When you're working on your sense of humor, keep this fact in mind and write down your observations. If you can get a laugh out of day-to-day happenings, you can make a bigger laugh out of it for others.

However, **delivery** is key, which is why studying comedians and practicing in the mirror are so important.

Utilize Social Savviness

It's easy to be the life of the party by cracking jokes. But humor, however useful, just isn't appropriate on all occasions. You have to be sensitive to the mood of a gathering to discern whether a joke is appropriate or not.

If you crack jokes at the wrong time, people are going to see you as insensitive, and that will alienate you very quickly.

The problem is, jokers often don't know when to stop.

This is why a lot of comedians have trouble with true, interpersonal connections. They're insensitive to moments when empathy, kindness, or seriousness are more fitting.

A sense of humor is important, but the ability to adjust to the direction of a conversation is paramount.

This is the same thing mentioned earlier, when we discussed paying attention to people's moods or personal preferences. When the other person is in a volatile or sensitive mood, levity is more likely to alienate them than calm them.

Mental flexibility, the ability to see where a discussion is going and the ability to adapt to the new direction, is a social skill you have to have in order to navigate relationships and build lasting and fruitful connections.

<u>Exercise</u>: Record What's Interesting About You

With that said, there are many simple things you can do to practice. Nothing is required but a willingness to try to be a better-rounded person.

One method used fairly frequently by counselors when they're trying to build a person's self-esteem is "journaling."

It doesn't have to be an hour-by-hour journal that records every trivial thing that happens, it's just a place to jot down anything you feel like recording.

Start by writing up a list of interesting or noteworthy facts about yourself. It's not bragging. You're not showing this list to anyone, you're just making an honest assessment of your positive assets.

You might list some physical attributes, but it'll be better to focus on easier talking points, such as your career, your personality, or other characteristics. A physical attribute isn't going to be as easy to discuss without sounding conceited.

For <u>example</u>, your list could read as follows:

1. Smart
2. Witty
3. Great college education
4. State championship for track in high school
5. Have 3 kids who are all doing well in school
6. Good cook
7. Speak Spanish fluently
8. Lost 60 lbs. 5 years ago
9. Took care of sick aunt when she was dying
10. Pretty hair

This list is diverse. It consists of a variety of things, not all focused on one specific attribute.

You're making this list, essentially, to help start up conversations. It should be diverse enough that you can talk to pretty much anyone at any time.

For example, if you wanted to connect with someone who has children, you'd bring up your own. If the other person happened to be athletic, you might mention that you'd had experience in track before, or that you'd managed to lose weight by exercising.

The point here is to get, on paper, a list of your different skills, knowledge, or experiences that you can share with others.

Going back to your journal, you can also jot down interesting facts that you learn, news stories that you find interesting, the jokes mentioned above, or other notes about yourself or your life.

You can also use your journal as a place to keep track of questions you'd like to ask other people. They could be things you're curious about specific to an individual, or they could be general questions that could apply to anyone. If you keep these "in your back pocket" questions, however, make sure they're relevant to whoever you're speaking with.

If you're trying to connect with a businessman, for instance, he's probably going to be more interested in questions about education or important current events than in fad topics or movies.

For the most part, though, these questions could be about anything, such as:

1. Where did you go to school?
2. How many kids do you have?
3. Are you from this area?
4. Are you married?
5. What do you do for a living?
6. Did you see (insert name of movie here)?
7. Have you read about (current event)?

This list is pretty general, but it'll give you an opportunity to gain a lot of information about a person's interests.

You can keep this list for as long as you need to, but the idea is to eventually get to the point where you don't need it anymore.

Chapter 5
How to Keep a Connection

Once The Connection Is Made

This may be the hardest part of all...

Not all connections are created equal. In other words, and as we all know, some connections begin in the most opportune way possible, but after a while they become a struggle to keep afloat. So why do other connections work out so well? What's the factor that makes one relationship work and another flounder?

For example, if you are married, you know that marriage is a daily job. You have to wake up each day ready to work on your relationship with your spouse. You have to be able to put your relationship over everything life throws in your way.

The same goes for any relationship on any scale. Putting in work to keep a connection alive is vital for any friendship, romantic relationship, or work connection. You both have to be able to give and take and be able to make necessary allowances for each other.

Why should you bother?

Only <u>you</u> can answer that.

You need to value that relationship and what it brings to your life.

Look at your friendships:

- Do your friends make you laugh and give you good advice?

- Do they buy you dinner or set you up on dates?

- What do those people bring to the table in your world?

Consider this carefully, don't take them for granted.

Putting In Maintenance

In order to maintain connections, you have to continue to work on and incorporate all the skills you've read about here. That means that when your friend is boring you *(and they will at times, for sure)*, you've still got to "grin and bear it." That wasn't just a method for *making* the initial connection, it was a method for *maintaining* it as well.

This doesn't mean, however, that you're always going to be able to keep your relationships together. Remember, you're only half the equation. If the other person isn't committed, the connection is eventually going to peter out. And this does happen. People lose touch, go in separate directions, or grow apart all the time.

The thing is, in maintaining a relationship you can only be responsible for your own actions. Trying to rebuild a connection or strengthen a weakening bond means putting yourself out there, and it can be uncomfortable. It can be hurtful or frightening to watch a connection start to disintegrate.

The question is: *What can you do about it?* Well, look within and be honest with yourself.

This is another great use for your journal.

Write down your thoughts, feelings, or concerns in regard to the relationship, and then give it some genuine thought.

Try writing down questions specific to that person. Jot down jokes they'll find funny, or current events you feel they would be interested in discussing. You can devote whole pages to ideas for rebuilding the bridge between yourself and that person.

This may seem like a lot of effort...but everything worth having is worth working for, right?

You may be thinking, *"I want to connect with my co-workers or my boss, but I don't really want to have to wake up each day and worry about it."*

It may seem like a lot of investment, and you might feel that you shouldn't have to work this hard. However, the truth is, you'll have to invest in your work relationships if you really want to have success in your job. This doesn't mean *"schmoozing"* per se (although that can help).

Meet reality: You have to be prepared to smile, nod, *"fake it 'til you make it"*, ask questions, and show interest every day. Period. This isn't something you can do once, then throw in the towel. **It's a continuing responsibility.**

Chapter 6
Start Creating Connections Now

Past To Present

So, do you now have a good basis for establishing immediate connections? If you've really been paying attention, you should, and you should also understand why some people seem to be able to do it effortlessly.

You've seen how to break the ice or build a bridge between yourself and someone else, in a romance, work relationship, friendship, or anything else.

But the real lesson at hand is **valuing** the relationship *(or prospect of a relationship)* enough to work on it. This isn't always easy. It will require effort, but if you are aware of the true value the relationship has for you, it won't be as difficult as you might think.

The base factor for the entire job is the understanding that building connections is a learned skill. Just like learning to read and write.

Connecting The Dots

It may all seem like a bunch of random facts at first, but when you put them into practice and connect all the pieces, you'll be able to see a whole, healthy relationship emerge.

But you have to know, analyze, and work on yourself first!

Are you confident enough to show your best in the initial connection? Can the person see something to like or respect in your manner before he ever meets you, something that will make him desire a connection?

Can you respect the other person's feelings enough to show genuine interest in a conversation and work to keep it going, even when you find it less than enthralling?

Do you care enough to learn techniques that will gain the other person's interest, techniques such as humor and jokes? These are methods that are all about the other person. Can you go out of your way to learn to please others?

Once you've made the connection, will you work to keep the relationship strong?

A relationship may seem like a lot of work at times, but if you truly value it, you can be willing to practice these skills and be willing to put yourself out there to maintain it.

But if you keep going strong, it will all be worth it in the end!

An INSTANT Thank You!

Thank you for entrusting in the <u>INSTANT Series</u> to help you improve your life.

Our goal is simple, help you achieve instant results as fast as possible in the quickest amount of time. We hope we have done our job, and you have gotten a ton of value.

If you are in any way, shape, or form, dissatisfied, then please we encourage you to get refunded for your purchase because we only want our readers to be happy.

If, *on the other hand*, you've enjoyed it, if you can kindly leave us a review on where you have purchased this book, that would mean a lot.

What is there to do now?

Simple! Head over to http://www.instantseries.com, and sign up for our **newsletter** to stay up-to-date with the latest instant developments *(if you haven't done so already)*.

Be sure to check other books in the INSTANT Series. If there is something you like to be added, be sure to let us know for as always we love your feedback.

Yes, we're on **social medias**. *Don't forget to follow us!*

https://www.facebook.com/InstantSeries

https://twitter.com/InstantSeries

https://plus.google.com/+Instantseries

Thank you, and wish you all the best!
- ***The INSTANT Series Team***

Instant Connection